RUTH

FAITHFULNESS IN FAMINE

RUTH

FAITHFULNESS IN FAMINE

STORYTELLER

Lifeway Press®
Brentwood, Tennessee

Editorial Team

Cynthia Hopkins
Writer

Stephanie Cross
Associate Editor

Reid Patton
Senior Editor

Jon Rodda
Art Director

Tyler Quillet
Managing Editor

Joel Polk
Publisher, Small Group Publishing

Brian Daniel
Director, Adult Ministry Publishing

ISBN: 978-1-0877-8355-0 • Item number: 005842042
Dewey decimal classification: 222.35 • Subject heading: BIBLE / HISTORICAL BOOKS OF THE OLD TESTAMENT / RUTH

All Scripture quotations are taken from the Christian Standard Bible®, Copyright © 2017 by Holman Bible Publishers. Used by permission. Christian Standard Bible® and CSB® are federally registered trademarks of Holman Bible Publishers.

To order additional copies of this resource, write to Lifeway Resources Customer Service; 200 Powell Place, Suite 100, Brentwood, TN 27027; fax 615-251-5933; call toll free 800-458-2772; order online at Lifeway.com; or email orderentry@lifeway.com.

Printed in the United States of America

Adult Ministry Publishing • Lifeway Resources • 200 Powell Place • Brentwood, TN 37027

CONTENTS

ABOUT STORYTELLER

God could've chosen to reveal Himself in any way He desired, yet in His wisdom, He chose to reveal Himself in the context of a story. We come to know and understand this reality as we immerse ourselves in the Scriptures and begin to see the entirety of Scripture as one interconnected story. By becoming familiar with the individual stories of Scripture, we train ourselves to see each as one part of God's big story.

Storyteller: Ruth is a five-week devotional and group Bible study experience designed to take people through Scripture in a way that is beautiful, intuitive, and interactive. Each volume uses a book of the Bible or a portion of Scripture from within a book to examine a key theme. This theme guides the Bible study experience and gives readers handles to help understand and digest what they're reading.

At the end of each study, your should have a deeper understanding of God, His Word, the big themes of Scripture, the connectedness of God's story, and His work in your life.

Let's enter the story together.

ABOUT RUTH

SUMMARY

The book of Ruth is a beautiful story of faithfulness in famine. Naomi and her husband left the land God had promised to His people to find provision elsewhere in Moab—a land known for its worship of idols. The family settled there and their sons married Moabite women. Naomi's husband and two sons died in Moab, greatly expanding her understanding of the meaning of *famine*. Apart from two daughters-in-law, she had nothing and no one—or so she thought. One daughter-in-law, Ruth, became an ever-present demonstration of faithfulness and the means by which God would provide above and beyond anything either woman could possibly imagine. Leaving Moab and returning to Bethlehem, a city in the land God's promises, Ruth stepped forward in her newfound faith to gather leftover grain in a field. Unknown to her, that field belonged to Naomi's wealthy relative, Boaz. God was at work. In short order, Boaz faithfully fulfilled the role of family redeemer for Naomi and Ruth. Boaz married Ruth, and they had a child named Obed. Naomi's grandson Obed was God's provision for Naomi's security in the present and also for the future security of all God's people. Obed became the grandfather of David, whose descendant is Jesus Christ.

PURPOSE

A Gentile (non-Jewish) woman from a pagan nation who God involved in the earthly lineage of the one and only Messiah shows God's heart for all people from every nation. A broken woman from the chosen nation who God provided for shows His ever-present care for those who follow Him. The book of Ruth shows, in every human condition and circumstance, that God is faithful and trustworthy to ultimately answer uncertainties with hope and redemption for those who trust in Him.

CIRCUMSTANCES

Ruth takes place "during the time of the judges" (1:1), when "everyone did whatever seemed right to him" (Judges 17:6). This was a period of great moral decline among God's people. Chapter one begins with famine in Bethlehem, which may very well have been the result of Israel's rebellion.

AUTHOR AND DATE

The book of Ruth does not indicate its author. However, the Talmud (Jewish tradition) attributes its writing to the prophet Samuel. The events detailed in Ruth took place around 1100 BC, near the time that Samuel was born. The genealogy included at the end of Ruth shows us that it was written later, at some point after David was anointed as the king of Israel (1050 BC).[1]

---

1. Adapted from: Iain M. Duguid, "Ruth," in *CSB Study Bible: Notes*, ed. Edwin A. Blum and Trevin Wax (Nashville, TN: Holman Bible Publishers, 2017), 401.

SIMPLIFIED OUTLINE OF RUTH

Moab (1:1-22)	Elimilech's family departs for Moab. Death and despair lead Naomi and Ruth to decide to return to Bethlehem.
Fields of Bethlehem (2:1-23)	Ruth meets Boaz, who then provides for Naomi and Ruth.
Boaz's Threshing Floor (3:1-18)	God provides instructions to build the tabernacle so that He may dwell with His people.
City of Bethlehem (4:1-22)	Boaz marries Ruth, who then gives birth to Obed, blessing Naomi with a new family. With Obed's birth, Ruth becomes an ancestor of David.

TIME FRAME OF EVENTS

Problems in Moab (1:1-5)	Ten years
Provision in Bethlehem (1:6–4:12)	Two months
Provision in God's Plan of Redemption (4:13-22)	First year of marriage, conception and birth of Obed

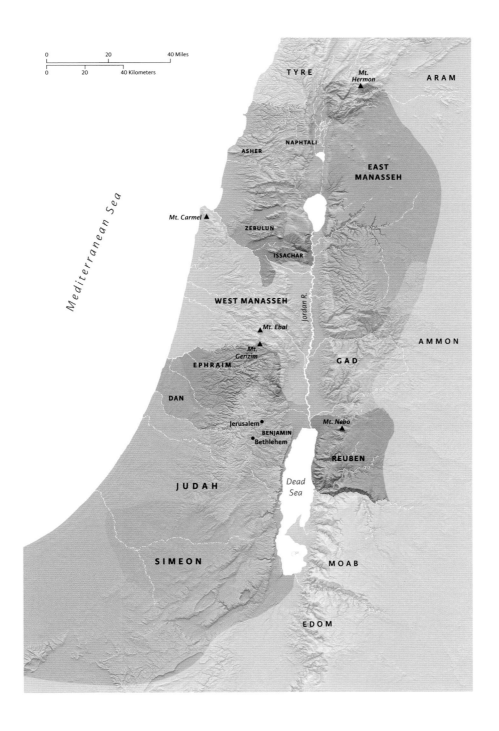

0   20   40 Miles

0   20   40 Kilometers

Mediterranean Sea

TYRE

Mt. Hermon ▲

ARAM

ASHER

NAPHTALI

EAST MANASSEH

Mt. Carmel ▲

ZEBULUN

ISSACHAR

WEST MANASSEH

Jordan R.

▲ *Mt. Ebal*

▲ *Mt. Gerizim*

EPHRAIM

GAD

AMMON

DAN

Jerusalem ●

Mt. Nebo ▲

BENJAMIN

● Bethlehem

REUBEN

JUDAH

Dead Sea

SIMEON

MOAB

EDOM

WHY STUDY RUTH?

From Genesis to Revelation, God reveals Himself through miracles. In those same pages of Scripture, He reveals Himself in the routine and ordinary events of daily life—and far more often. To this point, the book of Ruth serves as a beacon of hope in our most mundane moments. There are no outright miracles in Ruth, yet few books of the Bible help us see God's sovereignty, grace, and provision so clearly. In our loss, our grief, and even our bitterness, He is at work.

But it is not only God's provision in the day-to-day of earthly life that Ruth demonstrates. The bigger picture is that sin causes every person a spiritual famine of the soul. And in our famine, whatever specific circumstances it entails, God is faithful. Loss, grief, and bitterness are part of the story, but they are not the final story—God brings eternal rescue.

Over five weeks, we will walk together through the four chapters of Ruth, confronted simultaneously by the depth of human suffering and the breadth of God's faithfulness in that suffering. Ruth's story gives us certainty about our own. All of history and all of your life—the miraculous and the mundane—points to full and final redemption in Jesus Christ.

HOW TO USE THIS STUDY

Each week follows a repeated rhythm to guide you in your study of Hebrews and was crafted with lots of white space and photographic imagery to facilitate a time of reflection on Scripture.

The week begins with an introduction to the themes of the week. Throughout each week you'll find Scripture readings, devotions, and beautiful imagery to guide your time.

WEEK 1

BROKEN

Each week includes five days of Scripture reading along with a short devotional thought and three questions to process what you've read.

The Scripture reading is printed out for you with plenty of space for you to take notes, circle, underline, and interact with the passage.

The sixth day contains no reading beyond a couple of verses to give you time to pause and listen to what God has said through the Scriptures this week. You may be tempted to skip this day all together, but resist this temptation. Sit and be quiet with God—even if it's only for a few minutes.

The seventh day each week offers a list of open-ended questions that apply to any passage of Scripture. Use this day to reflect on your own or meet with a group to discuss what you've learned. Take intentional time to remember and reflect on what the story of Ruth is teaching you.

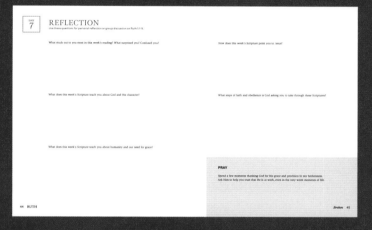

Throughout each week of study, you will notice callout boxes or supplemental pages provided to give greater context and clarity to the Scripture you're reading. These features will help you connect Ruth to the bigger story of Scripture.

LEADING A GROUP

Each week of study contains a set of questions that can be used for small group meetings. These open-ended questions are meant to guide discussion of the week's Scripture passage. No matter the size of your group, here are some helpful tips for guiding discussion.

PREPARE

REVIEW the Scripture and your answers to the week's questions ahead of time.

PRAY over your group as well as the Scriptures you've been studying. Ask God's Spirit for help to lead the group deeper into God's truth and deeper in relationship with one another.

MINIMIZE DISTRACTIONS

We live in a time when our attention is increasingly divided. Try to see your group time as a space and respite from the digital clutter—from scrolling, notifications, likes, and newsfeeds. Commit to one another to give focused time and attention to the discussion at hand and minimize outside distractions. Help people focus on what's most important: connecting with God, with the Bible, and with one another.

ENCOURAGE DISCUSSION

A good small group experience has the following characteristics.

EVERYONE IS INCLUDED. Your goal is to foster a community where people are welcome just as they are but encouraged to grow spiritually.

EVERYONE PARTICIPATES. Encourage everyone to ask questions, share, or read aloud.

NO ONE DOMINATES. Even though you may be "leading" the group, try to see yourself as a participant steering the conversation rather than a teacher imparting information.

DON'T RUSH. Don't feel that a moment of silence is a bad thing. People may need time, and we should be glad to give it to them. Don't feel like you have to ask all the questions or stay away from questions that aren't included. Be sensitive to the Holy Spirit and to one another. Take your time.

INPUT IS AFFIRMED AND FOLLOWED UP. Make sure you point out something true or helpful in a response. Don't just move on. Build community with follow-up questions, asking other people to share when they have experienced similar things or how a truth has shaped their understanding of God and the Scripture you're studying. Conversation stalls when people feel that you don't want to hear their answers or that you're looking for only a certain answer. Engagement and affirmation keeps the conversation going.

GOD AND HIS WORD ARE CENTRAL. The questions in this study are meant to steer the conversation back to God, His Word, and the work of the gospel in our lives. Opinions and experiences are valuable and can be helpful, but God is the center of the Bible, the center of our story, and should be the center of our discussion. Trust Him to lead the discussion. Continually point people to the Word and to active steps of faith.

KEEP CONNECTING

Spiritual growth occurs in the context of community. Think of ways to connect with group members during the week. Your group will be more enjoyable the more you get to know one another through time spent outside of an official group meeting. The more people are comfortable with and involved in one another's lives, the more they'll look forward to being together. When people move beyond being friendly to truly being friends who form a community, they come to each session eager to engage instead of merely attending. Reserve time each week to touch base with individual group members.

WEEK 1

BROKEN

Trust that God is at work.

The beginning of Ruth makes us think the book is a horrible tragedy. The middle makes us think it is a beautiful love story. In the end, we discover it is both.

In fact, Ruth's story is a gospel story.

Ruth lived during the time of the judges, when God's people weren't acting at all like God's people. Their motto wasn't all that different from one we hear today. People in Israel were "living their truth," believing that whatever seemed right to a person was, in fact, right for that person.

And there were consequences.

The tragedy that unfolds in the first verses of Ruth illuminates the brokenness of humanity—through the perspective of a single family. Sin's effects are ever-present in the world, not just in a global sense, but in every single, solitary life. Yet, at the very same time, God is at work.

As Ruth's story unfolds, we will see that the tragedy of sin and its consequences are met with grace and provision from God. Ruth's story will reveal to us the extent of God's grace. This is good news, because the God we meet in the book of Ruth is exactly who God is throughout time and circumstance. No matter what's happening in our lives, God meets us there and draws us to Himself.

But to participate with Him in that story, we must first recognize our brokenness.

RUTH 1:1a

¹ During the time of the judges, there was a famine in the land.

JUDGES 21:25

²⁵ In those days there was no king in Israel; everyone did whatever seemed right to him.

A FAMINE OF THE SOUL

Faithfulness is a personal choice we each must make.

Joshua knew it, and at the end of his earthly life, he said it out loud. The Israelites needed to make a choice: who they would serve—the One true God who keeps every promise or the pagan gods of the world whose promises are only shadows (see Joshua 24:15). At Joshua's call, the people agreed to serve the Lord, but that choice didn't last. Within a generation, they had once again lost their way.

This is the spiritual context in which Ruth takes place. This famine didn't occur in a time when God's people were faithfully following Him. This wasn't a "Why do bad things happen to good people?" type of situation. The book's opening phrase, "During the time of the judges," informs us that the events in Ruth took place during one of the darkest times in Israel's history, when "Everyone did what seemed right to him."

In other words, all people had chosen their own way instead of God's way. They were sinning and unrepentant—and they were facing the consequences of those choices. It is likely that the famine was part of God's judgment on His people for abandoning Him to worship other gods (see Judges 2:11-15).

The situation in Ruth informs us about our own: what *seems* right to us is wrong. We all have sin in our lives that carries unavoidable and devastating consequences—a famine of the soul that ends in certain death. We are broken in a way that no improvement of circumstance can fix.

Yet, as we will see across the pages of Ruth's story, God faithfully provides the way. And the call to turn to Him in faith remains, even the darkest, most difficult days.

You are broken in a way that no improvement of circumstance can fix.

REFLECTIONS

What was the underlying problem in "the time of the judges"?

What choice did God's people have in the famine of Ruth 1:1?

How do Judges 21:25 and Ruth 1:1a apply to your life? What choices have been placed before you?

INSIGHTS

The story of Ruth is more than a story about a broken girl who meets a heroic boy and lives happily ever after. It, like every book in the Bible, is a story about God's plan to rescue every person from the brokenness of sin through the life, death, and resurrection of the one and only true Hero of the world—Jesus Christ. We should not wait until the end of the book of Ruth to consider Jesus as part of the story. He is the central point of the story from verse 1. We need a Savior, and God's plan in every circumstance throughout history is to redeem us.

RUTH 1:1-2

1 During the time of the judges, there was a famine in the land. A man left Bethlehem in Judah with his wife and two sons to stay in the territory of Moab for a while. ² The man's name was Elimelech, and his wife's name was Naomi. The names of his two sons were Mahlon and Chilion. They were Ephrathites from Bethlehem in Judah. They entered the fields of Moab and settled there.

DISTANT AND DISPLACED

"It seemed like a good idea at the time." You've probably heard someone say those words, or you may have even said them yourself. It's a popular expression used to voice regret over a decision made with good intentions that ended up having bad results. And if Elimelech had the opportunity to speak on his own behalf in Ruth, he might choose those same words.

That's the thing about sin—it very often seems right. In Elimelech's case, it may have even seemed necessary. We don't know much about his family's exact situation, but there was famine in Bethlehem. Famine in any context causes apprehension. Even the remote possibility of scarcity causes us to race to the grocery store to hoard our favorite snacks. This was worse. Bethlehem (literally "House of Bread" in Hebrew) was named after bread, but there was no bread to be found.

It is likely that Elimelech exhausted numerous potential solutions before packing up and moving to Moab. In taking this view, we can assume the best that Ruth allows. But we should not confuse Elimelech for Abraham. The latter was willing to faithfully follow God into uncertain territory. The former was unwilling to faithfully remain in the very land Abraham sacrificed everything for God's people to receive. Elimelech turned his back on God's promises and took his family to live among God's enemies.

The hard truth we must consider is that we are more often like Elimelech than we are like Abraham.

Instead of faithfully going or staying wherever the Lord leads us, we are prone to go to those places that seem right in our circumstances—and *settle* there. Brokenness, then, is a byproduct of our sin. Void of prayerful consideration and obedience to God's commands, acting on what seems like a good idea distances us from God and displaces us from our purpose among His people.

You will be tempted to go to those places
that seem right—and settle there.

REFLECTIONS

What does Elimelech's willingness to move his family from Bethlehem to Moab reveal about his faith?

Elimelech only planned to stay in Moab "for a while." Are sinful choices justified if we commit them only "for a while"? In what situations have you been tempted to think that way?

What are your "fields of Moab," those places you have settled that invite distance from God?

TRACING THE STORY

Elimelech's decision to move must be understood in light of the long held hostility between Israel and Moab. The origin of the Moabites was a horrific low point in Israel's history (see Genesis 19:36-37). And their story of resistance, seduction, and oppression had only continued to bring additional low points for God's chosen people, to the point that Moab was excluded from the assembly of the Lord (see Deuteronomy 23:3-6; Numbers 22–24; 25:1-9; Judges 3:15-30).

RUTH 1:3-5

[3] Naomi's husband, Elimelech, died, and she was left with her two sons.
[4] Her sons took Moabite women as their wives: one was named Orpah and
the second was named Ruth. After they lived in Moab about ten years,
[5] both Mahlon and Chilion also died, and the woman was left without her
two children and without her husband.

VULNERABLE AND ALONE

The situation in the first five verses of Ruth moves from bad to worse to tragic.

After distancing and displacing his family, Elimelech died. Whatever dreams he had peddled that Naomi began to embrace along the way to Moab were quickly lost. Naomi found herself a single mom in a strange place where there was no natural spiritual or relational community for her to find like-minded friends. There were no Hebrew women for her sons to marry, and Jewish law prohibited them from marrying Moabites, since Moabites served other gods (see Deuteronomy 7:3-4).

We don't know how long it was just the three of them, but they continued to do what seemed right in their own eyes. Mahlon and Chilion took Moabite wives named Ruth and Orpah, and the family settled in Moab for ten years. They made a life there—this was no longer a temporary visit.

But before any new dreams of life in Moab could gain traction, both Mahlon and Chilion died. Now, Naomi was experiencing heartache and loss with the added difficulty of being a widow. In those days, widows were among the most vulnerable people in society. Naomi had limited resources, no financial stability, no descendants, and no hope for the future. Elimelech's choice to do what seemed right to him eventually resulted in the death of 75 percent of his family and what seemed like worse than death to the rest.

Naomi's story is included in the pages of Scripture for this very reason. For us to understand the gospel's power in our lives, we must come to terms with our desperate need—a need that only God can remedy. Earthly dreams hold no promise. When we do what seems right in our own eyes and make a life for ourselves there, it moves from bad to worse to tragic. Romans 6:23 explains it like this: "For the wages of sin is death." In other words, eternal death is the eventual outcome of every sin.

But Romans 6:23 also offers the hope that Ruth will ultimately illuminate: "but the gift of God is eternal life in Christ Jesus our Lord." Apart from Christ, you are wholly vulnerable and alone in the consequences of sin. But in Christ, you are wholly protected and embraced in the power of God's faithfulness and love.

Earthly dreams hold no promise.

REFLECTIONS

What potential reasons are there to explain why Naomi and her two sons stayed in Moab after Elimelech died?

What are some temporary solutions you have made for problems that turned into something permanent? What has God taught you through that experience?

What role and responsibility do we have as believers in Christ when it comes to continuing faithfully in tragic circumstances?

RUTH 1:6-7

RUTH'S LOYALTY TO NAOMI

⁶ She and her daughters-in-law set out to return from the territory of Moab, because she had heard in Moab that the Lord had paid attention to his people's need by providing them food. ⁷ She left the place where she had been living, accompanied by her two daughters-in-law, and traveled along the road leading back to the land of Judah.

GRIEF AND GRACE

Sometimes when life hits hard, you just want to go home.

Naomi was in that place. She'd given Moab a full decade of her life, and it couldn't have been worse. There was no end to her troubles in sight, either. Living in a foreign land without a husband or sons, the situation was precarious. Naomi and her two daughters-in-law didn't have anything to their names or a way to provide for themselves. In those days, women went from the care of their fathers to the care of their husbands. If a woman's husband died, his family was responsible for providing another male relative for her to marry—that is, if the woman was still of age to be married and have children.

This was not the case for Naomi, Orpah, and Ruth. They left Moab to return to Bethlehem for food, not husbands. Naomi had heard things were looking up again in Judah and, as risky as a journey like that would have been, the three women began the long trek over rough and steep terrain back to Bethlehem.

To this point, people have been the subject of the book of Ruth—terribly flawed people at that. In verse 6, we see the first sign of God at work among them. In their grief, God showed grace.

There was grace in the hearing. In Naomi's state of mind and heart, it was a gift of God that she could hear and perceive good news of any kind.

There was grace in the physical aid. This was still the period of the judges, when people "did whatever seemed right" (Judges 21:25) in their own way of thinking. Yet God provided food in the famine.

And He provided that food for His people (see v. 6). There was grace in the loyalty God showed to disloyal people, in the keeping of the covenant with covenant-breakers.

Naomi's attitude hadn't yet caught up with her physical movement, but God was leading her home, to the place of redemption. And He does the same for us. In our brokenness, God's grace draws us toward our home with Him.

In your brokenness,
God's grace draws you home.

REFLECTIONS

After the devastating decade in Moab, where Naomi lost everything, why would she risk the dangers of traveling back to Bethlehem?

What have you expected of God during times of intense grief?

What grace has God shown you in those times?

God in Our BROKENNESS

The Lord is explicitly recognized only briefly in this week's passage. However, God's presence and activity is central to Ruth's story. Every detail in Ruth connects to the bigger story of Scripture—God faithfully reaching into our brokenness to draw us back to Him. To see how the story of Ruth echoes the whole story of Scripture, consider these passages that align with this week's reading.

RUTH 1:1a

God responds to human rebellion.

PROVERBS 14:12; ROMANS 5:12; ROMANS 8:20-21

RUTH 1:1b-2

God's discipline is for our ultimate good.
Any attempt to escape it is continued rebellion.

PSALM 139:7-8,23-24; ROMANS 8:23-25; HEBREWS 12:5-13

RUTH 1:3-5

God's commands are not arbitrary. There is no sin
where circumstance absolves us of consequence.

DEUTERONOMY 7:1-4; 1 SAMUEL 15:22; 1 CORINTHIANS 15:34; GALATIANS 6:7-8

RUTH 1:6,8-9

God provides in our brokenness.

PSALM 34:18; PSALM 146:5-9; 2 TIMOTHY 2:13

RUTH 1:7

In our brokenness, God invites us to return to Him.

JOB 22:23a; ZECHARIAH 1:3; LUKE 15; ROMANS 2:4

RUTH 1:8-9

[8] Naomi said to them, "Each of you go back to your mother's home. May the Lord show kindness to you as you have shown to the dead and to me. [9] May the Lord grant each of you rest in the house of a new husband." She kissed them, and they wept loudly.

DAY 5

WITHDRAWAL AND WEEPING

Where verses 6-7 offer our first hint of hope in Ruth, verses 8-9 quickly return us to the depths of despair. It's no surprise, though. That's the way grief goes.

In her brokenness, Naomi was surely grateful for Ruth and Orpah's empathetic presence. Initially, she may have thought the three women could get through it together. Theirs were hands to hold. But as Naomi walked along the road, she began to emotionally withdraw. As an older woman far from home, her situation was different. She decided to carry the burden alone.

Thinking Ruth and Orpah's only shot at any future happiness was to return to their fathers and try to remarry in Moab, Naomi told them to go home. And according to every standard at the time, Naomi wasn't wrong. It had cost her everything to leave home, and she didn't want Ruth and Naomi to continue down the same tragic path. Naomi thought the two young women still had lives worth living— even if she didn't.

The brokenness of their lives hit them hard in that moment. Naomi was releasing their hands from holding hers any longer, and they wept.

They wept for the tragedy of death in their families. They wept because things didn't turn out how they imagined. They wept because they were enduring ongoing personal trauma. They wept in deep compassion for one another. They wept because it all seemed so unfair.

Can you relate? When we realize our brokenness—whether because of personal sin or sin's effects in the world—God meets us in the middle of it all (see Psalm 34:18). And as His people, we are called to meet each other there too (see Romans 12:15). We are tempted to withdraw in our weeping, but God invites us to connect and unite. The truth is, we are all broken people. Together, we will see and believe He is at work.

The Lord meets you in the
middle of your brokenness.
You can meet others there too.

REFLECTIONS

What do Naomi's words in verses 8-9 demonstrate about her belief in God even in the worst of times?

When you are feeling broken, do you tend to withdraw from God and people or connect and unite with God and people? Why?

Why does healing from brokenness require us to connect and unite with God? Why does healing from brokenness require us to connect and unite with other people emotionally, socially, physically, mentally, and spiritually?

PAUSE & LISTEN

Spend some time reflecting over the week's reading.

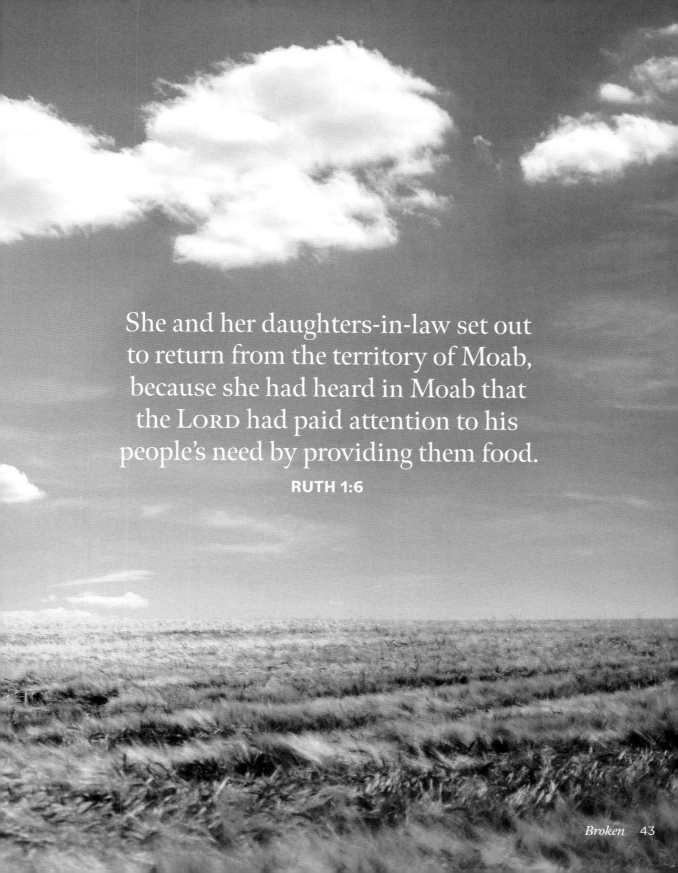

She and her daughters-in-law set out to return from the territory of Moab, because she had heard in Moab that the LORD had paid attention to his people's need by providing them food.

RUTH 1:6

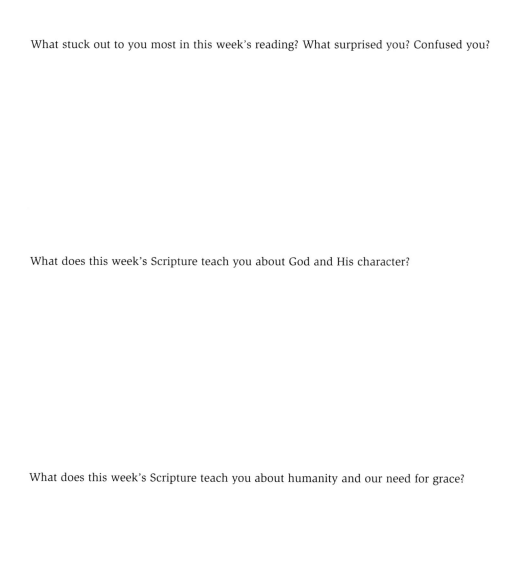

DAY

7

REFLECTION

Use these questions for personal reflection or group discussion on Ruth 1:1-9.

What stuck out to you most in this week's reading? What surprised you? Confused you?

What does this week's Scripture teach you about God and His character?

What does this week's Scripture teach you about humanity and our need for grace?

How does this week's Scripture point you to Jesus?

What steps of faith and obedience is God asking you to take through these Scriptures?

PRAY

Spend a few moments thanking God for His grace and provision in our brokenness.
Ask Him to help you trust that He is at work, even in the very worst moments of life.

WEEK 2

EMPTY

Walk by faith.

Brokenness is a state that defines every one of us, and that brokenness brings every one of us to the point of decision—will we walk in faith, trusting God to restore us as He promises, or will we walk in our brokenness, emptied of hope altogether?

Contrary to what we might think, there are no other options.

The second half of Ruth's first chapter illuminates this truth for us. Strangely, though, it was not the Hebrew woman who stepped forward in faith. Instead, a Moabite— who most likely had only come to know about God in recent years—stood alone to declare her allegiance to God and walk in faith, no matter how hard it might be.

Her insistence in this decision serves as an example to us.

As we continue reading Ruth's story, we will be challenged to meet our own brokenness with faith in God—however uncommon that may be. We will be reminded that it isn't only pagan idolaters who live as those who are hopeless: in brokenness and grief, we all face that temptation.

The world upholds personal dreams, practicality, and self-care as the surest producers of happiness. Elevating faith in God above those seems senseless to most and is imagined as a sure path to emptiness wherever fullness is defined by the identities we create ourselves.

At the very same time, God is working to bring about His good and loving purposes in the lives of those who choose to walk by faith. And He will complete that work. Are you ready?

RUTH 1:10

[10] They said to her, "We insist on returning with you to your people."

<table><tr><td>DAY
8</td><td># AN INSISTENCE OF NEED</td></tr></table>

Grief can make us feel as if we are on a roller coaster of emotions—shock, denial, guilt, pain, anger, worry, emptiness, and even relief. Naomi surely experienced the ups and downs of these emotions and more, but at the point of verse 10, she had settled into a place of bitter resignation. Frequent mood swings were no more. Naomi was ready to embrace her emptiness—alone.

But her intention was not shared. The two daughters-in-law, who were each facing their own moments of soul-crushing personal crisis, intended to leave everything and everyone in Moab behind.

Why would they do that? Why would Ruth and Orpah disagree with such kind and sensible instruction? Why would they "insist" on going with Naomi to Bethlehem?

We might reason that it was simply an act of compassion. After all, as an older widow traveling in a foreign land, Naomi's situation was the worst by far. But this was not lending a hand on moving day, picking up the tab at dinner, or buying a bag of groceries. In following Naomi to Bethlehem, Ruth and Orpah intended to give their *lives*.

The most likely explanation? They had seen in Naomi's family something they lacked. All three women innately understood there was something missing, and they saw a glimmer of hope in the one true God. But Ruth and Orpah had never known anything else. Until Elimelech, Naomi, Mahlon and Chilion entered their lives, they had lived fully immersed in Moabite culture, with no understanding of the God who saves.

What was true for these women is true for us all—we either insist on following the Lord or insist on making life complicated. The former brings us fullness, and the latter will ultimately leave us empty.

So Ruth and Orpah wept at the thought of leaving Naomi and insisted on going with her to the land of promise. They wanted to join with God and be a part of His people.

Insist on following the Lord.

REFLECTIONS

What do Ruth and Orpah's insistence of going with Naomi to her people tell you about where they had placed their hope?

What actions do you need to take to ensure that your relationship with the Lord takes precedence over everything else?

What might this insistence of faithfulness cost you?

RUTH 1:11-13

[11] But Naomi replied, "Return home, my daughters. Why do you want to go with me? Am I able to have any more sons who could become your husbands? [12] Return home, my daughters. Go on, for I am too old to have another husband. Even if I thought there was still hope for me to have a husband tonight and to bear sons, [13] would you be willing to wait for them to grow up? Would you restrain yourselves from remarrying? No, my daughters, my life is much too bitter for you to share, because the Lord's hand has turned against me."

CLOUDED JUDGMENT

When we consider what seems right to us, acting in faithfulness to God often seems senseless.

That's why Naomi doubled down. Ruth and Orpah's insistence in following her to Bethlehem lacked practicality, and it made Naomi uncomfortable. In her view, she had already wrecked their lives enough—it was time to part ways. She had appealed to their emotions with no success (vv. 8-9), now she would appeal to logic.

Naomi believed the two younger women would give up any hope of future husbands and children if they followed her to Bethlehem. And in that day and culture, few would disagree. Naomi had no husband, no sons, and no expectation for any of that to change. On top of that, it was unlikely that any husband worth having in Bethlehem would be interested in marrying Moabite women. So she wanted them to know she had nothing left to offer them.

When we consider Naomi's argument in its entirety, we can understand her settled perspective to be, "I believe the Lord will show kindness to Ruth and Orpah, but not if I'm in the picture. God is clearly done with me." She thought God was against her. Willingly walking under that curse and sharing in her bitterness didn't make any sense—not when Ruth and Orpah had other options.

Naomi's brokenness had given way to emptiness. She thought she had nothing left to give. God was providing for His people in Bethlehem, but Naomi had become so bitter that she couldn't believe that provision would extend to her. The only truth she could really give attention to was her own despair, and it clouded her judgment to the point that she advised Ruth and Orpah to return to their pagan gods.

We all face that same danger. Brokenness is never allowed in our lives apart from God's provision and invitation to turn to Him for healing. But our sin and our human nature want us to allow bitterness to cloud our judgment of brokenness, making us think we have nothing left to give. When we do that, we won't give at all. Instead, we will do the exact opposite—we will point others away from God.

Faithfulness is never senseless.

REFLECTIONS

If Naomi had been thinking clearly, from a place of faith and not bitterness, how might she have advised Ruth and Orpah differently?

What act of faith has God called you to that doesn't make sense from a practical, logical perspective?

How is God using Ruth's story to speak to you about that?

INSIGHTS

When an Israelite husband died, his brother or near relative was to marry the widow and continue the brother's name (see Deuteronomy 25:5–10). Learn more about this on day 22 (page 111).

RUTH 1:14-15

[14] Again they wept loudly, and Orpah kissed her mother-in-law, but Ruth clung to her. [15] Naomi said, "Look, your sister-in-law has gone back to her people and to her gods. Follow your sister-in-law."

THE SUBTLETY OF FAITHLESSNESS

Though Orpah steps out of the story here and makes way for Ruth to become the heroine, none of us think of her as a villain. She isn't.

Naomi had laid out a convincing argument for both women to go back to Moab. Orpah saw wisdom in Naomi's words and decided to turn back. Ruth held on, firm in the decision she had already made. From verse 14, we can see that neither made their decision easily.

On the surface, there didn't seem to be one right answer, and we can understand both perspectives. We can even sense some of same turmoil we have in making many of our own major decisions. *Should I take this job or that one? Should I move here or there?*

Those types of decisions aren't always a choice between faithfulness and faithlessness. And we can argue that Orpah wasn't necessarily turning her back on God. She could have returned to her people and continued to follow God. But as much as that argument might seem right to us, verse 15 lets us know the reality of what was taking place. Naomi told Ruth to follow her sister-in-law "back to her people and to her gods."

This wasn't merely a choice of practicality, though Naomi and Orpah had settled it in their minds as such. Orpah was turning away from God. Although she is not a villain, she serves for us as a caution. The choice between following God or following idols is often subtle. A lack of faith doesn't always look like a lack of faith on the surface.

The world will persuade us to make our practical lists, identifying the pros and cons that help us choose what path to follow. But God operates outside the realm of human wisdom and earthly practicality. He is calling us—even when we are broken and empty—to follow Him and Him alone, no matter what contrary advice we reason or receive.

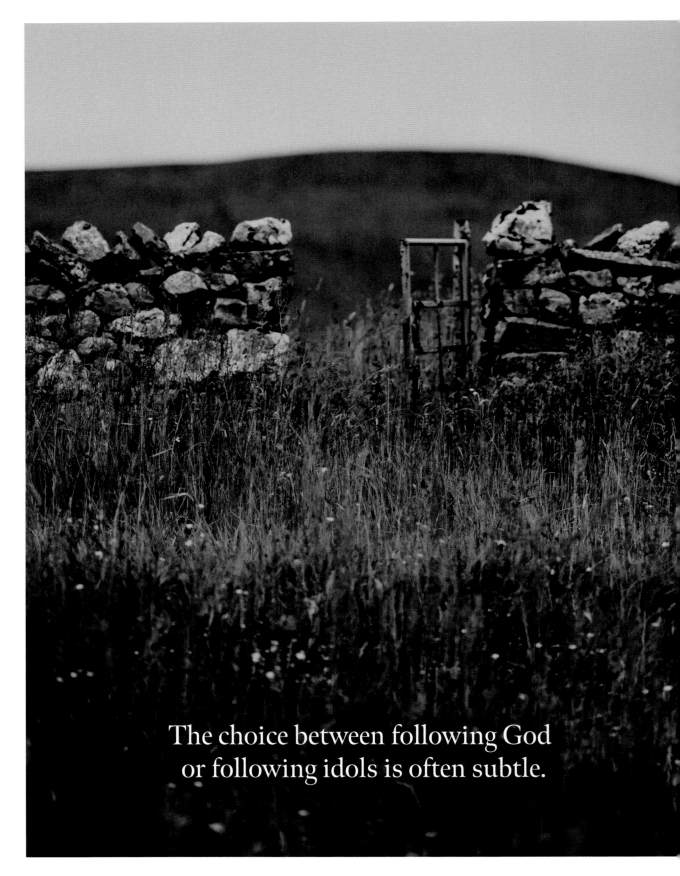

The choice between following God
or following idols is often subtle.

REFLECTIONS

What was the new reason for Orpah's weeping and kiss?

Does this mean Orpah's expression of commitment to follow Naomi in verse 10 was insincere? Why did she change her mind?

When have you wavered in your commitment to follow the God through difficulty? What happened?

INSIGHTS

Jesus also indicated the subtlety of the world's call to faithlessness. In Matthew 7:13-14, He instructs us this way: "Enter through the narrow gate. For the gate is wide and the road broad that leads to destruction, and there are many who go through it. How narrow is the gate and difficult the road that leads to life, and few find it." The way that seems right to most people will ultimately be revealed as devastatingly wrong.

RUTH 1:16-17

[16] But Ruth replied:

> Don't plead with me to abandon you
>
> or to return and not follow you.
>
> For wherever you go, I will go,
>
> and wherever you live, I will live;
>
> your people will be my people,
>
> and your God will be my God.

[17]
> Where you die, I will die,
>
> and there I will be buried.
>
> May the LORD punish me,
>
> and do so severely,
>
> if anything but death
>
> separates you and me.

A LINE IN THE SAND

Ruth had every earthly reason to turn around and head back to Moab with Orpah. Naomi had relieved her of responsibility, saying in as many ways as she knew how, "Don't come to Bethlehem. I don't want you there."

That's what makes what happened next extraordinary. The flow of the text gives us the sense that the weeping ended, and Ruth locked eyes with Naomi to state her personal choice in no uncertain terms. And that choice was one of astonishing loyalty and commitment.

Ruth's words speak to us. They have become ornamental decor to commemorate weddings and express deep friendship. "Where you go I will go, and where you stay I will stay" is engraved on necklaces and painted as wall art—and rightly so. Ruth's commitment to Naomi serves as a model of love for us to follow.

But the commitment Ruth was making goes far beyond human relationship.

Her Hebrew mother-in-law was bitter, empty, and feeling abandoned by God (see v. 13). Yet this young Moabite widow confidently decided, "Your God will be my God" (v. 16).

We don't know when Ruth first believed in the God of Israel. It is likely that she had made that commitment previously, perhaps as her husband or mother-in-law told her about the one true God. But here in this moment, Ruth drew a line in the sand for herself. When Naomi's doubts could have easily swayed her to turn away, Ruth confirmed her decision to trust God—and that decision informed every other decision Ruth would make.

Life sets before each of us that same choice. In bitter circumstances, we will either be swayed by the world to turn away from God, or we will confirm our decision to trust Him. Faith doesn't look away from God to find another answer; it looks to God as the only answer.

Faith looks to God as the only answer.

REFLECTIONS

What stands out to you as most extraordinary in these two verses?

What is a situation for which you need determination to trust God? How does Ruth's story help you?

How is Ruth's statement in verses 16-17 a picture of what happens when we turn to God through faith in Jesus Christ?

GOD

in our emptiness

Before Naomi comes on the scene in God's story, we read numerous examples of God's faithfulness in experiences of both literal and metaphorical famine. Naomi overlooked that history, but we should not. Remembering what God has done reminds us that He is always at work in the lives of His people. He is faithful to turn every tragedy into triumph.

The Fall
GENESIS 3:1-13,16-19

The Promise
GENESIS 3:15,22-24

The Flood
GENESIS 6:5-7,11-13,17

The Covenant
GENESIS 6:8-9,18-19; 8:1,15-18; 9:1-17

Abraham's Testing
GENESIS 18:10-14; 22:1-2

The Blessing
GENESIS 21:1-3; 22:9-18

Joseph's Betrayal
GENESIS 37:14-28,36; 39:7-20

The Provision
GENESIS 45:4-8; 50:20

Oppression in Egypt
EXODUS 1:8-22

The Exodus
EXODUS 3:7-10; 14:21-31

RUTH 1:18-21

[18] When Naomi saw that Ruth was determined to go with her, she stopped talking to her.

[19] The two of them traveled until they came to Bethlehem. When they entered Bethlehem, the whole town was excited about their arrival and the local women exclaimed, "Can this be Naomi?"

[20] "Don't call me Naomi. Call me Mara," she answered, "for the Almighty has made me very bitter. [21] I went away full, but the Lord has brought me back empty. Why do you call me Naomi, since the Lord has opposed me, and the Almighty has afflicted me?"

DAY 12 | MISPLACED FOCUS

After such a beautiful declaration of loyalty (see vv. 16-17), we might expect more hugging and crying. We can imagine Naomi being overcome with gratitude as she realized what a tremendous gift Ruth was. We might think Ruth's loving sacrifice would help Naomi's grief progress into a place of hopeful acceptance.

But that's not what happened. Naomi walked those fifty miles to Bethlehem in complete silence, and her bitterness grew.

The faith of the Moabite shone brightly as the faith of the Israelite faltered. As Ruth stepped forward courageously in faith, Naomi stumbled forward in hopeless defeat. Ruth was ready to see her circumstances in light of her identity in God's family. Naomi was ready to see her circumstances as the defining mark of her identity.

Pleasant (Naomi) became bitter (Mara).

To understand God's message in this part of the story, it is important to note that Naomi didn't question God's existence. She believed in His omnipotence and sovereignty (see vv. 20-21). She understood that tragedy in life is a consequence of sin, whether it be her own or the pervasive state of life on this sin-cursed earth. But she allowed her circumstances to shape her perception of the rest of the story.

Focusing on her loss, Naomi accepted her circumstances as her own personal Egyptian oppression, forgetting that God is able to part the waters toward freedom.

It is possible for God's people—filled with knowledge of Him and a history with Him—to operate from a place of emptiness. That happens when we construct an identity based on our circumstances.

There is a better way! Even in the most hopeless situations, there is hope. As Naomi would soon learn, God is always at work. He will accomplish His *good* purpose in you. So fix your eyes on the signs of His goodness, mercy, and promise. Trust Him, and walk forward in faith.

Reject an identity based on your circumstances.

REFLECTIONS

List every evidence you find in Ruth 1:18-21 that Naomi was using her circumstances to interpret her identity.

How do you think these verses would have changed had Naomi interpreted her identity by God's love and promise of provision rather than her circumstances?

Is there a situation that has you operating from a place of emptiness? To walk forward in faith, what truth about God do you need to focus on in that circumstance?

PAUSE & LISTEN

Spend some time reflecting over the week's reading.

"Don't plead with me to abandon you or to return and not follow you. For wherever you go, I will go, and wherever you live, I will live; your people will be my people, and your God will be my God."

RUTH 1:16

REFLECTION

Use these questions for personal reflection or group discussion on Ruth 1:10-21.

What stuck out to you most in this week's reading? What surprised you? Confused you?

What does this week's Scripture teach you about God and His character?

What does this week's Scripture teach you about humanity and our need for grace?

How does this week's Scripture point you to Jesus?

What steps of faith and obedience is God asking you to take through these Scriptures?

PRAY

Confess to God your temptation to walk in empty bitterness when the circumstances of life take an unwelcome turn. Ask Him to help you remember His faithfulness in the past so that you might trust His faithfulness in the present and future.

WEEK 3

PROVISION

Expect God to exceed
your expectations.

Dorothy had it right: there's no place like home. For some, it means the comfort of a favorite meal shared with familiar faces, or the welcome consistency of plans and purpose. For others, though, home is a uniquely painful reminder that life was supposed to be different.

The latter view was Naomi's. Though there were familiar places and faces, the town of Bethlehem didn't have the power to right a full decade of wrongs—even if she clicked her heels three times.

The truth is, no change in circumstance or scenery has the power to give any of us the contentment we need. Any expectation that it might will leave us disappointed.

God wants to show us the better way:

> The one who lives under the protection of the Most High
> dwells in the shadow of the Almighty.
> **PSALM 91:1**

It's true—life is supposed to be different, but not in the way we might imagine. God wants us to find our home *in Him*. And when we do, His provision always exceeds our expectations.

Would Naomi realize it? Will we?

RUTH 1:22–2:3

²² So Naomi came back from the territory of Moab with her daughter-in-law Ruth the Moabitess. They arrived in Bethlehem at the beginning of the barley harvest.

RUTH AND BOAZ MEET

2 Now Naomi had a relative on her husband's side. He was a prominent man of noble character from Elimelech's family. His name was Boaz.

² Ruth the Moabitess asked Naomi, "Will you let me go into the fields and gather fallen grain behind someone with whom I find favor?"

Naomi answered her, "Go ahead, my daughter." ³ So Ruth left and entered the field to gather grain behind the harvesters. She happened to be in the portion of the field belonging to Boaz, who was from Elimelech's family.

CERTAINTY IN PROVIDENCE

DAY
15

Hindsight is 20/20. It is far easier to look back on a difficult situation and see where God was working than it is to confidently rest in His sovereignty in the heat of the moment. That explains the disconnect between Naomi's attitude in chapter one and the author's telling of her story.

We know Naomi didn't see it, and it is likely that Ruth didn't either, but both women would eventually look back and know without a doubt that God was carefully providing for their needs all along. In famine, He brought bread back to Bethlehem. In tragedy, He brought Naomi and Ruth to Bethlehem at the start of the barley harvest. In a time when people did whatever they thought was right, He preserved a godly man who was a relative of Elimelech.

God had plans for their future even while Naomi and Ruth were unaware.

But unawareness of God's sovereign provision doesn't prevent any of us from taking initiative to faithfully seek out that provision. God calls us to remain faithful in famine.

That's exactly what Ruth did. Even if everyone else was doing whatever seemed right in their own eyes, she was fully committed to the Lord. So, Ruth asked Naomi if she could initiate opportunity for provision through hard work. God had set the precedent for such situations. His people were meant to care for those among them who were vulnerable, and Ruth humbly accepted her position as such (see feature on the next page). However, she had no presumption. Ruth was willing to work hard with the simple hope that someone might graciously allow her to collect their leftovers.

God continued to provide. As Ruth headed off to gather fallen grain, she "happened" to find herself in the exact part of a field that belonged to Boaz, the godly man who was a relative of Naomi's dead husband, Elimelech.

What we can now know in hindsight with certainty, Naomi and Ruth were beginning to understand: Ruth wasn't lucky; she was faithful. And God graciously guided her with His provision along the way.

God's sovereign provision works with our faithful initiative to seek it out.

REFLECTIONS

What hints of God's providence and possible provision do you find in Ruth 1:22–2:3?

When has it been hard for you to see God's provision in a difficult circumstance? What has hindsight taught you about God's providence in your life?

What actions could you take to faithfully seek out God's provision in uncertain circumstances?

TRACING THE STORY

Naomi thought God was against her, but God has always cared for the vulnerable. In the Old Testament, He instructed His people to lovingly provide for aliens, widows, and orphans (see Leviticus 23:22; Deuteronomy 10:18–19; 24:17–21; 27:19). In the New Testament, He also sets the clear expectation for true believers in Jesus Christ to show love and enact provision for foreigners, orphans, and widows (see Hebrews 13:1-2; James 1:27).

RUTH 2:4-12

⁴ Later, when Boaz arrived from Bethlehem, he said to the harvesters, "The LORD be with you."

"The LORD bless you," they replied.

⁵ Boaz asked his servant who was in charge of the harvesters, "Whose young woman is this?"

⁶ The servant answered, "She is the young Moabite woman who returned with Naomi from the territory of Moab. ⁷ She asked, 'Will you let me gather fallen grain among the bundles behind the harvesters?' She came and has been on her feet since early morning, except that she rested a little in the shelter."

⁸ Then Boaz said to Ruth, "Listen, my daughter. Don't go and gather grain in another field, and don't leave this one, but stay here close to my female servants. ⁹ See which field they are harvesting, and follow them. Haven't I ordered the young men not to touch you? When you are thirsty, go and drink from the jars the young men have filled."

¹⁰ She fell facedown, bowed to the ground, and said to him, "Why have I found favor with you, so that you notice me, although I am a foreigner?"

¹¹ Boaz answered her, "Everything you have done for your mother-in-law since your husband's death has been fully reported to me: how you left your father and mother and your native land, and how you came to a people you didn't previously know. ¹² May the LORD reward you for what you have done, and may you receive a full reward from the LORD God of Israel, under whose wings you have come for refuge."

<table>
<tr><td>DAY
16</td><td></td></tr>
</table>

SHELTER OF GRACE

All Ruth knew was she had found a field where she was allowed to pick up grain the harvesters dropped. She was surely thankful for that small provision, but God was still at work! As Ruth was hunched over, staring at the ground to gather whatever scraps she could find, Boaz arrived at his field and stopped to greet his workers.

His words and actions quickly let us know this was a man who made himself available to be used by the God.

After articulating kindness and concern both for his harvesters and the stranger working behind them, Boaz moved to action. He instructed the men to not harass her and extended to Ruth an open invitation to keep gathering grain in his field and to drink from the water jars as she did.

In a time when women weren't noticed—especially those who were foreign, widowed, and poor—Ruth was *seen*. And she wondered why.

Her question wasn't cynical. Ruth wasn't expecting Boaz to have ulterior motives. Instead, Boaz's generosity sent Ruth facedown to the ground in awestruck wonder.

Why was she being shown such grace? Why are we? Because that's what happens when we seek refuge under God's wings! He sees us, shelters us, and provides for our deepest needs.

God's provision is a gift of grace that changes the way we live. Seeking refuge under God's wings is not passive. We should not equate positioning ourselves in His care with curling up in a ball to simply out wait a crisis. No, seeking refuge under God's wings implies trust, and trust implies faithfulness.

Ruth's faithfulness to the Lord on Naomi's behalf moved Boaz to demonstrate faithfulness to the Lord on Ruth's behalf. And God would continue to provide—not because they worked hard, but because they took refuge in Him alone.

God sees you, shelters you, and provides
for your deepest needs.

REFLECTIONS

What does this section of Ruth teach you about God?

Are you ever tempted to believe God doesn't truly see you in your struggle? Why? What does Ruth 2:4-12 encourage you to do when you feel that way?

How should we answer Ruth's deeper question? Why has anyone found favor with God?

INSIGHTS

In Psalm 57:1, David echoed the figurative language of Boaz in Ruth 2:12. Hiding from Saul in a cave, David prayed, "I take refuge in you. I will seek refuge in the shadow of your wings until danger passes." But we shouldn't picture David passively waiting for the danger to pass! Like Ruth, David's faith took action. He trusted God and prayed fervently: "I call to God Most High, to God who fulfills his purpose for me" (v. 2).

RUTH 2:13-18

[13] "My lord," she said, "I have found favor with you, for you have comforted and encouraged your servant, although I am not like one of your female servants."

[14] At mealtime Boaz told her, "Come over here and have some bread and dip it in the vinegar sauce." So she sat beside the harvesters, and he offered her roasted grain. She ate and was satisfied and had some left over.

[15] When she got up to gather grain, Boaz ordered his young men, "Let her even gather grain among the bundles, and don't humiliate her. [16] Pull out some stalks from the bundles for her and leave them for her to gather. Don't rebuke her." [17] So Ruth gathered grain in the field until evening. She beat out what she had gathered, and it was about twenty-six quarts of barley. [18] She picked up the grain and went into the town, where her mother-in-law saw what she had gleaned. She brought out what she had left over from her meal and gave it to her.

DAY
17

BEYOND EXPECTATION

Believing God is good on an intellectual level is one thing. Sometimes, though, we experience God's goodness in a way that leaves us amazed—and changed forever. That is God's plan for all people, and it was God's plan for Ruth here in chapter 2.

Ruth left Naomi that morning empty-handed, hoping to somehow find enough morsels of grain to make it another day. She returned that night, grateful and surprised and with a full belly, a new job, and enough grain to last the two women several weeks.

This was more than a good day at work.

Boaz's generosity and kindness was far more than Ruth, or anyone in her position, could have imagined. He had given her a spot at the dinner table, and she was given so much that she couldn't finish. Afterward, Boaz instructed his workers to drop more grain behind them as they harvested that evening so that Ruth could gather more. By the time work wrapped up for the evening, she had six and a half gallons of barley and a take-out box of leftovers—which she somehow hoisted on her shoulder and carried back to town.

Boaz was a good guy. But as we will soon see, that's not really the point of the story. Boaz served for Ruth, Naomi, the harvesters—and all who caught wind of these events in the fields of Bethlehem that day—as a picture of God's kindness and generous provision. He serves in that same way for us today too.

God "is able to do above and beyond all that we ask or think according to the power that works in us—[for His] glory in the church and in Christ Jesus to all generations, forever and ever" (Ephesians 3:20-21). God is not only able, but He also does it! *Generous* is too small a word to describe Him. God pours out His goodness and grace in excess of all expectation, providing for our needs in surprising ways that we don't have the capacity to imagine.

God pours out His goodness in
a way that will leave you amazed.

REFLECTIONS

In what ways does Boaz's kindness toward Ruth reflect God's kindness toward us?

What effect do you imagine the sight of Ruth carrying home, in one day, multiple weeks of provision would have on Naomi's bitterness? What impact should it have on our bitterness?

Have you experienced God's goodness in a way that leaves you completely amazed and forever changed? How so? How might God use that experience to influence other people in your life?

RUTH 2:19-23

¹⁹ Her mother-in-law said to her, "Where did you gather barley today, and where did you work? May the Lord bless the man who noticed you."

Ruth told her mother-in-law whom she had worked with and said, "The name of the man I worked with today is Boaz."

²⁰ Then Naomi said to her daughter-in-law, "May the Lord bless him because he has not abandoned his kindness to the living or the dead." Naomi continued, "The man is a close relative. He is one of our family redeemers."

²¹ Ruth the Moabitess said, "He also told me, 'Stay with my young men until they have finished all of my harvest.'"

²² So Naomi said to her daughter-in-law Ruth, "My daughter, it is good for you to work with his female servants, so that nothing will happen to you in another field."

²³ Ruth stayed close to Boaz's female servants and gathered grain until the barley and the wheat harvests were finished. And she lived with her mother-in-law.

REALIZATION OF FAITHFULNESS

Naomi's response to the news that Boaz was the man who provided for them reveals much. When Ruth left that morning, Naomi had low expectations. She believed God was against her and Ruth was foolish for staying by her side (see 1:11-13). The narrator of the story identified Boaz as a relative of Elimelech (see 2:1), but Naomi hadn't mentioned him, although we learn she was aware of such men (2:20).

Her words in verse 20 help us understand why. Naomi didn't expect any of her husband's relatives to fulfill their God-given responsibilities. After all, she believed God had abandoned her, Elimelech, and their sons. Carrying that belief forward, it made sense to her that none of Elimelech's relatives would come to their aid. Naomi expected God to allow her to continue in her bitterness.

But God is faithful. He was working to awaken Naomi to new understanding of His faithfulness, and the light of realization began to flicker.

She could not explain away God's provision, nor did she try. Instead, Naomi told Ruth, "Yes, Boaz's kindness is good. Work in his field." And we see the first sign of grief give way to hope.

God's abundant provision continued in this way until the barley and wheat harvests ended. Ruth gathered grain in Boaz's field alongside the female servants, and each day she returned home, Naomi was confronted by one clear truth—God had not abandoned her; He was working.

For ten long years, Naomi lived in Moab feeling defeated. She returned to Bethlehem, and in just seven weeks (that's how long the harvests lasted), God reshaped her understanding of who He is. What an encouragement for us to wait for the Lord in seasons of sadness! The psalmist expresses it best: "Weeping may stay overnight, but there is joy in the morning" (Psalm 30:5).

God actively works to awaken
you to His faithfulness.

REFLECTIONS

What surprising information did Naomi receive from Ruth? What evidence is there in the passage that Naomi's bitterness toward God was dissolving?

When you look back over your life, how can you see God's providence there? Where was He working even when you couldn't see it at the time?

How has God surprisingly awakened your heart to new understanding of His faithfulness?

God's Provision Goes Above and Beyond

In this week's study we were reminded that we should never allow our circumstances to lower our expectations of God's character and activity. Ephesians 3:20 assures us that His power and will far exceed human understanding: God "is able to do above and beyond all that we ask or think according to the power that works in us." This truth finds its ultimate fulfillment in Jesus Christ, as the book of Ruth will show.

Read these verses and notice the connection to provision and grace from God.

"Seek first the kingdom of God and his righteousness, and all these things will be provided for you."

MATTHEW 6:33

"Give, and it will be given to you; a good measure—pressed down, shaken together, and running over—will be poured into your lap. For with the measure you use, it will be measured back to you."

LUKE 6:38

"A thief comes only to steal and kill and destroy. I have come so that they may have life and have it in abundance."

JOHN 10:10

"God is able to make every grace overflow to you, so that in every way, always having everything you need, you may excel in every good work."

2 CORINTHIANS 9:8

"Every good and perfect gift is from above, coming down from the Father of lights, who does not change like shifting shadows."

JAMES 1:17

RUTH 3:1-6

3 Ruth's mother-in-law Naomi said to her, "My daughter, shouldn't I find rest for you, so that you will be taken care of? ² Now isn't Boaz our relative? Haven't you been working with his female servants? This evening he will be winnowing barley on the threshing floor. ³ Wash, put on perfumed oil, and wear your best clothes. Go down to the threshing floor, but don't let the man know you are there until he has finished eating and drinking. ⁴ When he lies down, notice the place where he's lying, go in and uncover his feet, and lie down. Then he will explain to you what you should do."

⁵ So Ruth said to her, "I will do everything you say." ⁶ She went down to the threshing floor and did everything her mother-in-law had charged her to do.

THE RISK OF INITIATIVE

God's provision was unmistakable, and it woke Naomi from her spiritual slumber. The plan she set forth in chapter 3 was more than advice; it was a way of stepping into the work alongside Ruth, trusting God fully through obedience to all His commands.

From the beginning, Naomi had been concerned about Ruth's welfare—that hadn't changed. That's why she urged Ruth to return to her family in Moab, but now Ruth needed a different sort of urging. Naomi wanted her to know that faithfulness doesn't only involve hard work, it involves rest (see v. 1).

God's faithfulness in their famine was not a lesson on how to earn back His favor; it was a story of grace. But if they weren't careful, they might begin to think it was their hard work that would get them where they wanted to be.

The truth was that nothing in their lives had happened or would happen apart from the providential hand of God.

Just as faith does not force God's hand to reward us with health and wealth, neither does hard work. We should not sit idly by, waiting for God's kindness to come knocking. But hard work doesn't force God's hand to bless us either—it is a means by which God blesses us. The same is true for every other form of faithful obedience, including rest.

Naomi told Ruth how she could enter that rest, and it would again require initiative, as joining God in His purposes often does.

But the women would not circumvent His commands. Ruth agreed with Naomi's wisdom and determined to follow her counsel. In the expectation of provision, they would risk vulnerability and trust God to work it all out for their good.

Initiative often involves
vulnerability and risk.

REFLECTIONS

What is an area of faithfulness to God that you struggle to wholeheartedly accept, as Ruth did in verse 5?

What roles do risk and vulnerability play in that struggle?

In your experience, has joining God in His faithful provision required that you take initiative? Why?

INSIGHTS

Naomi's plan might seem odd to twenty-first century readers. There is likely cultural information that would increase our understanding of Naomi's plan, but we do not have that knowledge. However, we can see her plan in the very best light. Scripture gives every indication that Naomi and Ruth were women of integrity, offering an invitation of marriage to Boaz, who was a man of integrity. The plan was risky—Boaz could have misinterpreted the cues—but all parties involved were faithfully seeking God's will, and the women trusted in the character Boaz had shown them.

"May the LORD reward you for what you have done, and may you receive a full reward from the LORD God of Israel, under whose wings you have come for refuge."

RUTH 2:12

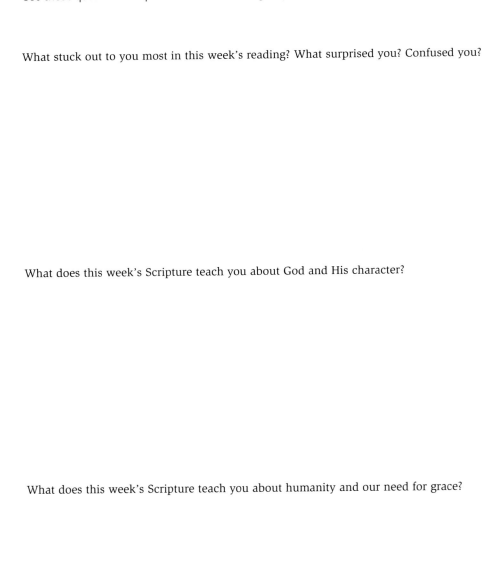

DAY
21

REFLECTION
Use these questions for personal reflection or group discussion on Ruth 1:22–3:6.

What stuck out to you most in this week's reading? What surprised you? Confused you?

What does this week's Scripture teach you about God and His character?

What does this week's Scripture teach you about humanity and our need for grace?

How does this week's Scripture point you to Jesus?

What steps of faith and obedience is God asking you to take through these Scriptures?

Spend a few moments thanking God in specific ways for His abundant provision. Spend a few more moments praising Him for the "home" you find under the refuge of His wings.

WEEK 4

REFUGE

Rest in God.

When you hear the word *refuge*, what comes to mind? Do you picture someone crouched under a rock formation during a raging storm, fleeing his or her country in hopes of a better life, or vacationing in an idyllic spot during a tough circumstance? When you need refuge, what do you do? Do you call a close friend, book a getaway, or get lost in a good book or TV series?

All of us find ways to escape the difficulties of life. The fact is, we can run away and sometimes we should. The problem is that our usual means of finding refuge are only temporary distractions. Every raging storm will subside, but others will eventually follow. That is true in every earthly context, whether we are at home in a favorite chair by the fire surrounded by family and friends or sitting in an oceanside cabana on a tropical island.

This side of heaven, it is impossible to escape brokenness.

True refuge is not a temporary distraction or short-lived solution. This is the message of Ruth, along with all of God's story. Trying to escape the famine by moving to Moab may have alleviated one problem, but another one soon came to Naomi and her family. In and of itself, Bethlehem didn't bring the refuge they needed, either. Naomi arrived home with a bitterness she couldn't shake. Even the abundant provision of grain Ruth had collected didn't end their struggle.

They couldn't escape or fix their brokenness, but they were learning that God is a constant shelter in brokenness.

Refuge is not found by running from our struggles; it is found by resting in God.

LEVITICUS 25:48-49

[48] he has the right of redemption after he has been sold. One of his brothers may redeem him. [49] His uncle or cousin may redeem him, or any of his close relatives from his clan may redeem him. If he prospers, he may redeem himself.

NUMBERS 27:11

[11] If his father has no brothers, give his inheritance to the nearest relative of his clan, and he will take possession of it. This is to be a statutory ordinance for the Israelites as the LORD commanded Moses."

<table>
<tr><td>DAY
22</td><td></td></tr>
</table>

A PRECEDENT FOR PROTECTION

If we're being honest, sometimes it doesn't seem like God is providing and protecting. Naomi lived in a world where men carried all the rights, and her husband and sons had died and left her alone in a foreign land. In Ruth, we see nothing but faithful kindness and diligence, and her husband died too. It makes us wonder why. After all, refuge is only needed if danger exists. But when things in the Bible don't seem to make sense, it doesn't mean Scripture doesn't make sense but that there is more to the story. In these times we may look to other parts of Scripture to expand our understanding.

Bad things do happen—and it grieves God. He did not sit idly by, unmoved by Naomi and Ruth's circumstance. No, He enacted His loving justice for their protection and provision in advance.

God had given instructions about what to do in such situations three hundred years before Naomi and Ruth came on the scene. When an Israelite became poor, then a "redeemer" was to step in and save the day. In Leviticus 25:25-27, Moses explained how this process should work. Similarly, Moses explained in Deuteronomy 25:5-6 that if a married man died childless, then his close relative was to take his wife and raise up a son in his name. This was important because land was considered a perpetual inheritance that was to stay in the family (see Numbers 27:7-11).

Without a redeemer, the poor Israelite was doomed to poverty and sometimes indentured service. Failing to fulfill the duty of a redeemer was considered a disgrace (see Deuteronomy 25:7-10), but fulfilling the role of a redeemer came at a cost. In all three of these situations, redeemers needed to shoulder the responsibility of their relatives and bear their burdens. The future hinged on the redeemer paying the price.

Ruth's story is our story. We are helpless in our own sin and in the circumstances we face from sin's effects. Our future hinges on the Redeemer paying the price, and He has. God enacted His loving justice to ensure our eternal safety in advance. In dying on the cross, Jesus redeemed, protected, and provided for us. Jesus is our Redeemer.

God enacted His loving justice for
your protection and provision.

REFLECTIONS

What does it teach you about God that He gave specific instructions on how to provide refuge for those in need?

When have you been tempted to think God was sitting idly by, unmoved by tragic circumstances? Why?

How has God already provided refuge for every circumstance you will ever face?

RUTH 3:7-9

[7] After Boaz ate, drank, and was in good spirits, he went to lie down at the end of the pile of barley, and she came secretly, uncovered his feet, and lay down.

[8] At midnight, Boaz was startled, turned over, and there lying at his feet was a woman! [9] So he asked, "Who are you?"

"I am Ruth, your servant," she replied. "Take me under your wing, for you are a family redeemer."

DAY
23

SMALL FAITH, BIG EFFECT

It's unlikely that anyone looked to Ruth as a spiritual giant. She had grown up in Moab, where the worship of false gods promised outcomes of land and fertility—yet Ruth had neither. She came to Bethlehem a childless widow, literally scraping by. Her closest friend was a bitter woman named Naomi, who was a shell of her former self.

From all appearances, Ruth had no reason for confidence in God. Any faith she had was surely no larger than the size of one of the small seeds of grain she gathered—and that was enough.

Following Naomi's advice, Ruth made her way to the threshing floor and laid down at Boaz's bare feet until he woke up and took notice. When he asked who was there, Ruth didn't just answer the who. She confidently answered the why by repeating his previous words to her back to him (see 2:12).

This young, heartbroken woman knew enough about God to understand that the wings of His refuge are often found in the help of His people. But it didn't stop at head knowledge—even the smallest amount of faith takes action.

Her plan was complex, but Boaz could understand her message in simple terms: "I'm done mourning. You're a family redeemer. Let's get married." Ruth had taken refuge in God, and Boaz had the ability to fulfill the blessing he wished for her. So that is what she asked him to do.

Time and culture makes it difficult for us to understand the meaning behind Ruth's actions, but we can certainly empathize with the anxiety she must have felt. It is hard to ask for help from other people. It can be hard to ask for help from God, and that's especially true when we've been wounded, but Ruth teaches us that God is faithful to give us refuge when we turn to Him. And turning to Him also means turning to His people.

Ruth's faith may have been small, but a small amount of faith has the potential to experience great effect (see Matthew 13:31-32)—because, whether we are spiritual infants or giants, God does not change.

REFLECTIONS

Why did Ruth have the confidence to make this bold request?

Why does Jesus often wait until we ask for help before He steps in to rescue us?

Based on your prayer life, how much confidence do you have in God? How does Ruth's story challenge you in this regard?

RUTH 3:10-14

[10] Then he said, "May the Lord bless you, my daughter. You have shown more kindness now than before, because you have not pursued younger men, whether rich or poor. [11] Now don't be afraid, my daughter. I will do for you whatever you say, since all the people in my town know that you are a woman of noble character. [12] Yes, it is true that I am a family redeemer, but there is a redeemer closer than I am. [13] Stay here tonight, and in the morning, if he wants to redeem you, that's good. Let him redeem you. But if he doesn't want to redeem you, as the Lord lives, I will. Now lie down until morning."

[14] So she lay down at his feet until morning but got up while it was still dark. Then Boaz said, "Don't let it be known that a woman came to the threshing floor."

DAY 24 | COMPLICATIONS

Naomi's plan seemed right, and Ruth successfully carried it out—so far. Boaz had the power and authority to redeem what death had stolen from the two women, and he was willing to exercise that power and authority. Even more, he *wanted* to marry Ruth.

But Boaz would only act as family redeemer in the right way. There was another man in the picture—a closer relative who could prevent Ruth from marrying Boaz. This other man could legally choose to take Ruth as his wife. This was no small obstacle; it was a problem that could cloud Ruth's vision moving forward.

Ruth maintained focus. She had grown to know and trust Boaz, and she remained at his feet for help (see v. 14).

Boaz wouldn't enter into her life any other way.

Ruth had options all along. She could have gone back to Moab and found a new husband there. In Bethlehem, she could have pursued another man who was younger, richer, or less concerned with what God and other people think. She could have forgotten all of it and carved her own path forward.

The choices before her could have complicated her decision, but Ruth was undeterred. In faith she trusted Boaz would redeem her, and she turned away from every other path.

This same principle is true in our own relationship with our Redeemer. The world offers us many choices that cloud our vision and complicate our decision to trust Jesus. It tempts us to think there are other ways.

All the while, Jesus calls out, "If anyone is thirsty, let him come to me and drink" (John 7:37), and "See! I stand at the door and knock" (Revelation 3:20). Jesus invites us to turn to Him for help, but He doesn't force His help on us. The choice is ours—where will we turn?

Jesus invites you to turn to Him for help.

REFLECTIONS

What complicated Ruth's path forward? What simple choice did Boaz encourage her to make?

What confidence could Ruth have as she waited through the night?

What circumstance tends to complicate your faith? What simple choice does Ruth's story encourage you to make?

TRACING THE STORY

The Hebrew Bible groups the books of the Old Testament in three sections: Law, Prophets, and Writings. These groupings order the books differently than our English Bibles, placing Ruth toward the end of the Old Testament, in the third and final section of Writings, after Proverbs. In fact, many scholars believe the book of Ruth came right after the book of Proverbs. Interestingly, the book of Proverbs ends with a description of a "wife of noble character" (31:10), and Boaz uses that exact same language to describe Ruth (see 3:11). Ruth is the kind of woman that Proverbs 31:10-31 describes.

RUTH 3:15-18

[15] And he told Ruth, "Bring the shawl you're wearing and hold it out." When she held it out, he shoveled six measures of barley into her shawl, and she went into the town."

[16] She went to her mother-in-law, Naomi, who asked her, "What happened, my daughter?"

Then Ruth told her everything the man had done for her. [17] She said, "He gave me these six measures of barley, because he said, 'Don't go back to your mother-in-law empty-handed.'"

[18] Naomi said, "My daughter, wait until you find out how things go, for he won't rest unless he resolves this today."

RESOLUTION PROMISED

From the time he first saw Ruth gathering barley in his field, Boaz provided for her needs. Recognizing her as a stranger, he hadn't judged her as irrelevant but took the time to learn her backstory (see 2:5). Seeing she was vulnerable, he hadn't left her to her own devices but invited her to work in his field under his protection (see 2:8-9). Sensing her hunger, he hadn't looked away but fed her a satisfying meal (see 2:14). Perceiving her shame, he hadn't let her leave with the small amount of grain she could gather but made sure she had a surplus (see 2:15-18). And understanding the complexity of her need, he hadn't shrugged his shoulders in helplessness, but promised to act in her behalf (see 3:11-13).

It was this abundance of generosity and kindness with which Ruth returned to Naomi after spending the night at Boaz's feet on the threshing floor. And Boaz's generosity and kindness hadn't run out. The six shovelfuls of grain in Ruth's shawl served as a promise that he would continue. Naomi understood. Her bitterness dissipated as she encouraged Ruth with confident expectancy—Boaz was working out the details. Another day would not pass without redemption.

Throughout the pages of Scripture, we see that God is in the details, actively working on our behalf. He doesn't judge us as irrelevant strangers but searches out the secrets of our hearts (see Psalm 44:21). He doesn't leave us to our own devices but strengthens and guards us from evil (see 2 Thessalonians 3:3). He doesn't leave us deficient but provides for every need (see Philippians 4:19). He doesn't shrug His shoulders in helplessness but fulfills His promise to redeem us now and for eternity (see John 3:16).

At the same time, our redemption is not yet complete, and sin threatens to cloud our vision. Naomi's words to Ruth, then, are instructive for us too—for now, we wait in trust that God is our refuge. Our Redeemer is at work to bring about the resolution He has promised. As He does, His mercies are new every morning—great is His faithfulness (see Lamentations 3:22-23)!

God is in the details, actively working on your behalf.

REFLECTIONS

What new attitude or belief do Naomi's words to Ruth in verse 18 reveal?

In what situation do you need to know God is actively working on your behalf?

What would it look like for you to faithfully "wait until you find out how things go" (v. 18)?

God Is Our Refuge

God is our refuge and strength,
a helper who is always found
in times of trouble.

PSALM 46:1

Ruth's story, as every other story told in the pages of Scripture, teaches us more about who God is and how relationship with Him affects daily life in the here and now. Note what Psalm 46 and other New Testament passages teach about life lived in God's refuge through relationship with His Son Jesus Christ.

When Jesus is our refuge, we can be . . .

. . . circumstantially unafraid.

RUTH 3:7
Ruth secretly approached Boaz in the night, uncovered his feet, and lay down.

PSALM 46:2-3; JOHN 14:27
We can face any difficulty without fear. Jesus gives us peace in this world.

. . . confidently dependent.

RUTH 3:9
Ruth turned to Boaz to take her under his wing for redemption.

PSALM 46:5a; 1 JOHN 5:4-5
We will not be overcome. Jesus has overcome the world.

. . . constantly helped.

RUTH 3:13-14
Ruth rested through the night, knowing that new mercy would come with the morning.

PSALM 46:5b; HEBREWS 4:15-16
God's help is as certain as the morning. Jesus gives His mercy and grace to meet our every need.

. . . contentedly restful.

RUTH 3:18
Ruth waited on Boaz to act in her behalf, knowing he wouldn't rest until her problem was resolved.

PSALM 46:10-11; TITUS 2:13
We can stop striving. We can rest knowing God is with us, Jesus will return, and He is right now working everything out for our ultimate good.

RUTH 4:1-8

RUTH AND BOAZ MARRY

4 Boaz went to the gate of the town and sat down there. Soon the family redeemer Boaz had spoken about came by. Boaz said, "Come over here and sit down." So he went over and sat down. ² Then Boaz took ten men of the town's elders and said, "Sit here." And they sat down. ³ He said to the redeemer, "Naomi, who has returned from the territory of Moab, is selling the portion of the field that belonged to our brother Elimelech. ⁴ I thought I should inform you: Buy it back in the presence of those seated here and in the presence of the elders of my people. If you want to redeem it, do it. But if you do not want to redeem it, tell me so that I will know, because there isn't anyone other than you to redeem it, and I am next after you."

"I want to redeem it," he answered.

⁵ Then Boaz said, "On the day you buy the field from Naomi, you will acquire Ruth the Moabitess, the wife of the deceased man, to perpetuate the man's name on his property."

⁶ The redeemer replied, "I can't redeem it myself, or I will ruin my own inheritance. Take my right of redemption, because I can't redeem it."

⁷ At an earlier period in Israel, a man removed his sandal and gave it to the other party in order to make any matter legally binding concerning the right of redemption or the exchange of property. This was the method of legally binding a transaction in Israel.

⁸ So the redeemer removed his sandal and said to Boaz, "Buy back the property yourself."

FIRST ON HIS MIND

As Ruth waited with her mother-in-law, Boaz waited at the city gate. When the man who had first right of refusal to buy Elimelech's property showed up, Boaz sat him down to lay out his options.

Having had much of the night and morning to discern the best course of action, Boaz thoughtfully formulated a plan. In front of the town's elders, he let the man know he had the first right to redeem the piece of land that had belonged to Elimelech. It wasn't until the man expressed his desire to possess the land that Boaz made any mention of Ruth—though she was certainly first on his mind.

The deal for Elimelech's land had two parts—the family redeemer could not take the land without also taking Ruth as his wife. Boaz's tact in laying out these facts in this order assures us he knew the second part would complicate the man's life. Maybe he was already married and had children whose inheritance would be compromised, or maybe the financial responsibility of Ruth and Naomi was more than he was prepared to accept. We don't know the specifics, but we do know marrying Ruth was a risk he wasn't willing to take.

Boaz was fully prepared to accept all responsibility as family redeemer. He had the right and the will to redeem Ruth—both were needed.

Why did God include details in the pages of Scripture about men doing business at the city gate and swapping sandals? In Boaz we see a picture of Jesus—one who has both the right and the will to redeem. At the gate of Bethlehem, God bound Himself to bring our Redeemer to Bethlehem—a thousand years before Mary and Joseph ever entered the story. Our redemption has always been in God's plan. There is no time, culture, or circumstance that can derail His intention to provide us refuge.

God has the right and the will to redeem.

REFLECTIONS

Based on Ruth 4:1-8, was Boaz was making decisions on the fly or had he developed a plan? Why does it matter?

What responsibilities did Boaz have to consider as he prepared to marry Ruth? What does this teach you about your relationship with Jesus, your eternal bridegroom (see Revelation 21:2)?

Apart from possessing one of Jesus's earthly sandals, can you have assurance in His redemption? How so?

INSIGHTS

In the time of the judges, removing one's sandal in this manner was an act of confirmation. Since there were no permanent records of court proceedings, witnesses were relied upon to recall transactions. The visual effect of removing a sandal made transactions more memorable. The meaning of the sandal probably originally signified sovereignty over property rights— one would be able to "walk" one's property (see Psalm 60:8; Joshua 1:3).

PAUSE & LISTEN

Spend some time reflecting over the week's reading.

So he asked, "Who are you?"

"I am Ruth, your servant," she replied.
"Take me under your wing, for
you are a family redeemer."

RUTH 3:9

REFLECTION

Use these questions for personal reflection or group discussion on Ruth 3:7–4:8.

What stuck out to you most in this week's reading? What surprised you? Confused you?

What does this week's Scripture teach you about God and His character?

What does this week's Scripture teach you about humanity and our need for grace?

How does this week's Scripture point you to Jesus?

What steps of faith and obedience is God asking you to take through these Scriptures?

PRAY

Pause and reflect on God as your refuge, both now in the circumstances of this world and in the future promise of eternity. Invite Him to show you any situation where you need to stop striving and rest in Him.

WEEK 5

REDEMPTION

Receive redemption.

The word *redemption* (in its various forms) appears twenty times in Ruth's four short chapters—and not because the writer lacked a thesaurus. The word *redemption* encapsulates the book's primary theme. Ruth, then, is no gospel side story; it is a beautiful picture of the gospel story.

In our brokenness and emptiness, God is about the business of redemption.

Though that message is woven throughout the pages of Ruth, the final chapter displays it most clearly. Ruth begins with death and ends with life. Her story moves from loss to gain, bitterness to joy, poverty to inheritance, hopelessness to hopefulness, and barrenness to blessing.

And so can yours.

God's provision isn't shortsighted. His refuge isn't temporary. He doesn't offer you help in one circumstance only to let you be defeated in the end. He pours out tangible reminders of His love and faithfulness with ultimate redemption always in mind.

God has the authority, power, and desire to save you and, throughout history, He has been working out the details.

Jesus Christ is *for you*. He longs for you to receive His redemption.

RUTH 4:9-10

[9] Boaz said to the elders and all the people, "You are witnesses today that I am buying from Naomi everything that belonged to Elimelech, Chilion, and Mahlon. [10] I have also acquired Ruth the Moabitess, Mahlon's widow, as my wife, to perpetuate the deceased man's name on his property, so that his name will not disappear among his relatives or from the gate of his hometown. You are witnesses today."

WITNESSES OF HIS GRACE

As a way of visible testimony, a sandal had been swapped. People saw the transaction that took place between Boaz and the other relative. But Boaz didn't want to leave anything up to human imagination. The act of redemption is a big deal, after all. There would be far-reaching effects. So, Boaz spoke up to make the exchange and his purpose in it clear.

In verses 9-10 we have record of his verbal testimony, made in the presence of many people who were gathered at the city gate. Boaz wanted them to know they were all witnesses of redemption. Everything death had stolen from Elimelech's family, Boaz would buy back. The widows would not be left impoverished in nameless perpetuity. Naomi's family line and inheritance would be preserved.

Boaz's responsibility was to redeem; everyone else's was to give witness to it.

Certainly there might have been rumblings around town in the days, weeks, and months to follow. It had all happened so fast. How did bitter Naomi's life turn around so quickly? Why would Boaz marry a Moabite? What had either of the two women done to deserve such extraordinary mercy and grace?

We can surely relate. Those types of questions echo our own as we consider the redemption Jesus freely gives. Can a person's life turn around so quickly? Why would God save a sinful person like him or her? What can I do to earn God's favor?

God knew the rumblings of the human heart, and like Boaz, He did not leave anything up to imagination. The cross and the empty tomb served as visible testimony, and afterward, Jesus appeared to many people to make His sacrifice and purpose clear (see 1 Corinthians 15:3-8).

Our questions about His grace have been answered. Scripture records Christ's own testimony and that of those who witnessed His act of redemption (see Luke 24:44-49; Ephesians 1:7-10). And now we give witness to His redemption too.

Your questions about redemption
have been answered.

REFLECTIONS

The deal had been done in verse 8. What additional benefit was there to Boaz's verbal testimony?

What questions about redemption have you had? How have the accounts in God's Word helped you answer those questions?

In what sense are you a "witness" of Christ's redemption (see v. 10)? What responsibility do you have as such?

RUTH 4:11-12

[11] All the people who were at the city gate, including the elders, said, "We are witnesses. May the Lord make the woman who is entering your house like Rachel and Leah, who together built the house of Israel. May you be powerful in Ephrathah and your name well known in Bethlehem. [12] May your house become like the house of Perez, the son Tamar bore to Judah, because of the offspring the Lord will give you by this young woman."

INSPIRING FUTURE HOPE

The witnessing of redemption inspires hope.

Remember this was a dark time in Israel's history. Throughout the period of the judges, morality among God's chosen people had been spiraling downward. If not yet sitting at rock bottom, they were very nearly there. The spiritual condition in Israel was about as bad as it could get.

As such, we might expect a response like, "That's so nice, Boaz. Hope it works out for you," followed by the buzz of skepticism and rolling eyes as people quickly dispersed. Yet there at the city gate in Bethlehem, the crowd expressed great hope.

A strong, anticipatory three-layer blessing materialized—full of faith and remembrance that, through this act of redemption, God could bring about more. They acknowledged what God had done to build His people and asked Him to do it again. The expectation of fertility for Ruth, honor for Boaz, and generational blessing for their future child came as they remembered God's faithfulness amid human faithlessness.

The crowd had noticed—Boaz and Ruth were not like everyone else, doing whatever seemed right to them. They were seeking the Lord. If God had blessed their ancestors, surely He would bless this couple even more.

The redemption witnessed at the city gate inspired hope for the future of Israel. As God gave fertility, honor, and blessing to this family who had determined to settle themselves firmly under His wings of refuge, all who knew them would certainly be blessed.

Redemption inspires you to live and pray with hope.

REFLECTIONS

Why might it have been difficult for people to anticipate God's blessings on Boaz and Ruth?

Based on your current prayer life, do you live with an expectation of hope for the future? Why?

How should Christ's act of redemption on the cross inform and inspire your prayers?

TRACING THE STORY

Leah and Rachel's marriages to Jacob came about through deception, and the two women related to each other in jealousy and conflict. Yet God blessed them and their maidservants with fertility, through which came the twelve tribes of Israel (see Genesis 29:16-30:24; 35:16-26; 49:28).

Perez was the twin son of Judah and his daughter-in-law Tamar's illicit affair, yet God blessed him with an unbroken line of male descendants over several generations. His lineage included Boaz and later King David (see Genesis 38; Ruth 4:18-22).

RUTH 4:13-16

[13] Boaz took Ruth and she became his wife. He slept with her, and the LORD granted conception to her, and she gave birth to a son. [14] The women said to Naomi, "Blessed be the LORD, who has not left you without a family redeemer today. May his name become well known in Israel. [15] He will renew your life and sustain you in your old age. Indeed, your daughter-in-law, who loves you and is better to you than seven sons, has given birth to him." [16] Naomi took the child, placed him on her lap, and became a mother to him.

DAY 31

RENEWING BROKEN HEARTS

Naomi had suffered for ten years in Moab. She had become bitter and completely hopeless that God would redeem her life. She couldn't see through the pain. She couldn't see that God was at work in the details—through the allegiance of a determinedly faithful young woman named Ruth and the preservation of a godly relative named Boaz.

And once those two came together under the prayers of many witnesses, it didn't take long at all for God to fulfill the promise of redemption.

Previously barren, Ruth gave birth to a son, and all the women in town recognized the great change God brought about in Naomi's life. He had not worked in a way she had expected or imagined—He had done something far better.

The gushing that came at the child's birth wasn't hyperbole. The extraordinary nature of the events that transpired cannot be overstated. God had indeed brought redemption to Naomi against all odds and in abundance. Ruth's love and faithfulness was more valuable and a greater blessing than Naomi could have asked or imagined.

Through it all, God was showing that every person is infinitely valuable to Him— empty and broken as we are.

That message continued to inspire future hope. The child God gave this family would renew Naomi's life. He would sustain her. And Naomi's heart broke through the bitterness and settled in belief.

Taking the child in her arms, she opened herself up to God's great love again.

You are infinitely valuable to God—
empty and broken as you are.

REFLECTIONS

Read verses 14-15 again. Considering this as a picture of Jesus as our Redeemer, what do you learn about Him?

Seven sons would have represented the ultimate life for a woman in that culture. What have you considered as the ultimate life for you? Why is Jesus better?

How can you know that you, though empty and broken, are infinitely valuable to God?

INSIGHTS

In that culture, sons were considered the ultimate blessing of God and seven was the number of completion. "Better to you than seven sons" means that Ruth's faithfulness was better for Naomi than an infinite number of sons and all the earthly security they would bring.

RUTH 4:17-22

[17] The neighbor women said, "A son has been born to Naomi," and they named him Obed. He was the father of Jesse, the father of David.

DAVID'S GENEALOGY FROM JUDAH'S SON

[18] Now these are the family records of Perez:

Perez fathered Hezron,

[19] Hezron fathered Ram,

Ram fathered Amminadab,

[20] Amminadab fathered Nahshon,

Nahshon fathered Salmon,

[21] Salmon fathered Boaz,

Boaz fathered Obed,

[22] Obed fathered Jesse,

and Jesse fathered David.

FROM DEATH TO NEW BIRTH

The structure of Ruth's story goes against the way we've been trained to see stories work, including our own. Life starts with birth and ends in death. The book of Ruth, though, begins with death and ends with a record of births (see 1:3-5).

With Jesus, the best is yet to come.

When Boaz announced his intention to redeem Ruth and Naomi, the people at the city gate prayed that God would bless their family for generations to come. Redemption reaches forward; it begins with broken pieces and makes a whole. The last few verses of Ruth assure us that God did bless their family in that way. And the New Testament reveals to us that redemption is still reaching forward, even today.

As amazing as it was, the marriage of Boaz and Ruth and the birth of their child wasn't the climax of the story. Those blessings pointed to a far greater blessing still to come—God's ultimate plan of redemption.

The impact of that redemption would bless more than one bitter widow and her pagan daughter-in-law. Ruth's story, like ours, is about so much more than personal circumstance. The child Obed would grow up and have a son named Jesse, who would one day learn that God had chosen his youngest son David, an unimpressive shepherd in a field, as Israel's king. And he would leave a legacy that would stretch to eternity.

Life does begin with birth, but sin's presence in the world marks every birth with death. The apostle Paul put it this way in Ephesians 2:1: "You were dead in your trespasses and sins." This is true of us all (see Romans 3:10). But praise God, death does not have the final word.

We are born in death, and redemption moves us forever forward in life.

Death does not have the final word.

REFLECTIONS

Ruth and Naomi are part of a much bigger story being told. From the genealogy in Ruth 4:18-22, what conclusions can you draw about that story?

Which word is a more accurate description of your present circumstance: *death* or *life?* Which word is a more accurate description of your attitude in that circumstance?

What does Ruth's story teach you about your story?

Jesus Is Our
REDEMPTION

The book of Ruth points us to Jesus our Redeemer, one thousand years before He was born. In doing so, it teaches us about the redemption we have in Him. Note the correlation between redemption in Ruth's story and the New Testament passages about redemption in Christ.

Jesus's redemption . . .

. . . rescues us from wrath.

RUTH 4:9-10
Boaz took the necessary steps to secure for Ruth and Naomi what death had taken.

1 PETER 1:18-19
Jesus offered Himself as a blood sacrifice to secure for us new life.

. . . bears witness to us and through us.

RUTH 4:2,11-12
Boaz secured witnesses to his act of redemption.

ACTS 1:8; ROMANS 8:16
Jesus sent the Holy Spirit to bear internal witness and empower external witness to our redemption.

. . . renews and sustains us.

RUTH 4:15
Ruth's son Obed renewed her life and sustained her in her old age.

2 CORINTHIANS 5:17; 1 PETER 1:3-5
God's Son Jesus gives us new life and keeps for us an eternal inheritance that can never be destroyed.

. . . gives us new purpose.

RUTH 4:16-22
Naomi turned from the past and moved forward to impact future generations.

MATTHEW 28:19-20; PHILIPPIANS 1:21
Jesus's death and resurrection drives us to turn from the past and move forward to impact future generations.

MATTHEW 1:1-16

THE GENEALOGY OF JESUS CHRIST

¹ An account of the genealogy of Jesus Christ, the Son of David, the Son of Abraham:

FROM ABRAHAM TO DAVID

² Abraham fathered Isaac,

Isaac fathered Jacob,

Jacob fathered Judah and his brothers,

³ Judah fathered Perez and Zerah by Tamar,

Perez fathered Hezron,

Hezron fathered Aram,

⁴ Aram fathered Amminadab,

Amminadab fathered Nahshon,

Nahshon fathered Salmon,

⁵ Salmon fathered Boaz by Rahab,

Boaz fathered Obed by Ruth,

Obed fathered Jesse,

⁶ and Jesse fathered King David.

FROM DAVID TO THE BABYLONIAN EXILE

David fathered Solomon by Uriah's wife,

⁷ Solomon fathered Rehoboam,

Rehoboam fathered Abijah,

Abijah fathered Asa,

⁸ Asa fathered Jehoshaphat,

Jehoshaphat fathered Joram,

Joram fathered Uzziah,

⁹ Uzziah fathered Jotham,

Jotham fathered Ahaz,

Ahaz fathered Hezekiah,

¹⁰ Hezekiah fathered Manasseh,

Manasseh fathered Amon,

Amon fathered Josiah,

¹¹ and Josiah fathered Jeconiah and his brothers at the time of the exile to Babylon.

FROM THE EXILE TO THE MESSIAH

¹² After the exile to Babylon

Jeconiah fathered Shealtiel,

Shealtiel fathered Zerubbabel,

¹³ Zerubbabel fathered Abiud,

Abiud fathered Eliakim,

Eliakim fathered Azor,

¹⁴ Azor fathered Zadok,

Zadok fathered Achim,

Achim fathered Eliud,

¹⁵ Eliud fathered Eleazar,

Eleazar fathered Matthan,

Matthan fathered Jacob,

¹⁶ and Jacob fathered Joseph the husband of Mary, who gave birth to Jesus who is called the Messiah.

A LARGER STORY

Ruth and Naomi's lives meant more than they thought they did.

All the stories of the Bible are really telling one big story. Ruth and Naomi's story ends with the birth of David, who would become king. David's story comes with the promise that a king like David would one day rule again. David's story asks us prepare our hearts for a better king. In Jesus, we're given a better king who promises redemption and eternal joy. His story is the one that unites all the other stories, weaving together the strands of each person's story for His ultimate glory and our ultimate good.

This is the purpose of the genealogies we find in Ruth 4 and Matthew 1. Naomi held her grandson and rejoiced that God had removed her bitterness. Imagine the increase of her joy had she also known that her grandson's grandson would be God's chosen king of Israel, and that his line would lead to the King of all kings, Jesus the Messiah.

If Ruth is the zoomed in picture, Matthew zooms out and takes a grand look at God's work throughout History. Matthew 1 is a bird's eye view: as God worked in Ruth and Naomi's lives, the cross of Christ was on His mind. In their very worst days, God was working to bring about redemption. *He always is.*

The genealogy of Jesus contains names and stories that are vast and varied. In His earthly lineage are patriarchs and pariahs, aged and adolescents, males and females, Jews and Gentiles, prosperous and penniless. To us, some names are familiar and others are foreign, but God knows and treasures them all.

The point is not in who we are or what we can do, only what we mean to God and how He includes us in His great purpose and plan.

Our lives mean more than we think they do. Jesus entered to story so that we could be certain His redemption reaches into our story.

Your life means more than you think it does.

REFLECTIONS

What titles did Matthew assign Jesus in verses 1 and 16? What is the meaning of each title?

Which people do you recognize in this genealogy? What do you know about them? Do any of the people on the list surprise you? If so, who and why?

Throughout all of those generations, God was paving the way for Jesus and proving Himself faithful to His people. What does this mean to your relationship with Jesus today?

INSIGHTS

Matthew began Jesus's genealogy with Abraham, the first person the Bible called a Hebrew (see Genesis 14:13), probably to assure his Jewish readers that Jesus was a Jew, a descendant of Abraham, the father of the Jewish people (see John 8:39). Luke's genealogy, however, goes back to Adam, emphasizing the universality of the gospel (see Luke 3:23-38).

PAUSE & LISTEN

Spend some time reflecting over the week's reading.

The neighbor women said, "A son has been born to Naomi," and they named him Obed. He was the father of Jesse, the father of David.

RUTH 4:17

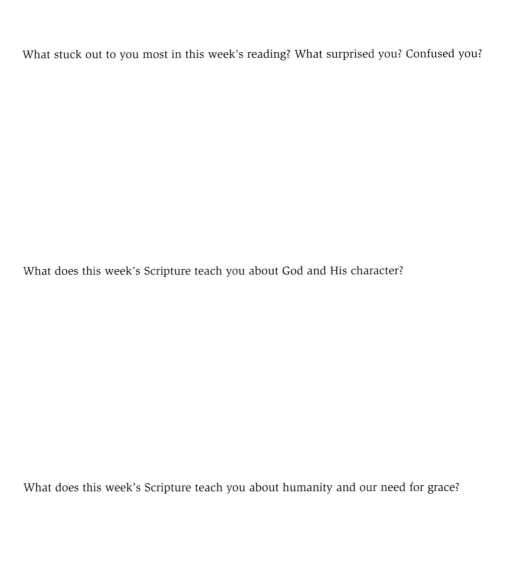

DAY
35

REFLECTION

Use these questions for personal reflection or group discussion on Ruth 4:9–22.

What stuck out to you most in this week's reading? What surprised you? Confused you?

What does this week's Scripture teach you about God and His character?

What does this week's Scripture teach you about humanity and our need for grace?

How does this week's Scripture point you to Jesus?

What steps of faith and obedience is God asking you to take through these Scriptures?

PRAY

Take a few moments to consider God's work throughout history to rescue you from sin. Thank Jesus for the gift of redemption. Ask Him to help you be a faithful witness of that gift.

PHOTOGRAPHY CREDITS

If only Solomon had written a book on wisdom.

Oh, wait.

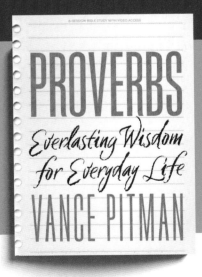

PROVERBS
Everlasting Wisdom
for Everyday Life
VANCE PITMAN

Take a month-long journey through all 31 chapters of Proverbs. You'll not only gain an appreciation for this popular and applicable book of the Bible, you'll also begin to develop a daily habit of seeking wisdom from God's Word. In addition to the four session videos, you get access to 31 short, daily teaching videos (one for each chapter), all included in the purchase price of the *Bible Study Book*.

Learn more online or call 800.458.2772.
lifeway.com/proverbs

Lifeway

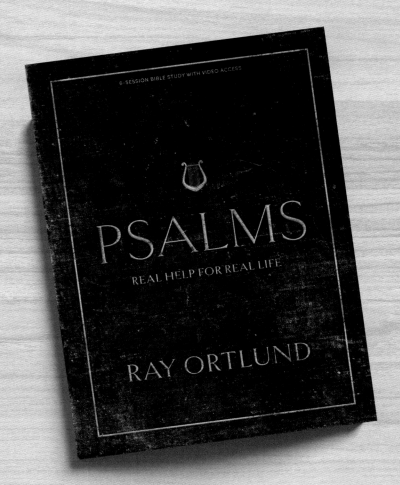

Learn to find help for all of life's circumstances.

The Psalms are filled with people venting surprisingly honest feelings toward God, whether it be anger, disappointment, awe, or happiness. This new study from Ray Ortlund will help you see that the Psalms are a place that God has provided to encounter Him and find help, rest, hope, courage, joy, and confidence for whatever you face in life.

EXPERIENCING
GOD

SOME STUDIES HELP YOU KNOW THE BIBLE.
THIS ONE HELPS YOU KNOW THE AUTHOR.

For more than three decades, God has used the truths of *Experiencing God* to awaken believers to a radically God-centered way of life. As a result, millions have come to know God intimately, to recognize His voice, and to understand His will for their lives. This new edition is revised, updated, and ready to lead you again—or for the very first time—into a deeper relationship with God.

Step into God's beautiful story.

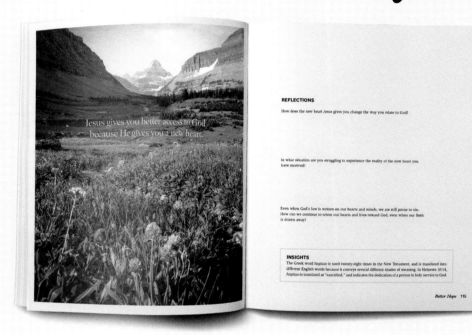

Storyteller is a Bible study series uniquely designed to be inviting, intuitive, and interactive. Each volume examines a key theme or story in a book of the Bible. Every week includes five days of short Scripture reading, a daily thought explaining each passage, a short list of questions for a group Bible study, and space for you to write down your discoveries. And new volumes are being added every year.

Learn more online or call 800.458.2772.
lifeway.com/storyteller

God is always at work.

When we meet Ruth, her husband has died and she is traveling with her mother-in-law to a land that is not her own. Though the circumstances seem dire, they are not beyond God's control.

The book of Ruth invites us to wait and hope along with the characters as we wait and hope for our redemption. Through Ruth we find a God who is always at work behind the scenes ready to show His faithfulness.

This six-session Bible study is designed to help you:

- Trust God when hope is hard to find
- Find the ways that God is working and connecting the smaller parts of your story to His bigger story
- See waiting not as a detour off the path but part of God's kindness and plan for you

ADDITIONAL RESOURCES

eBOOK
Includes the content of this printed book but offers the convenience and flexibility that come with mobile technology.

005842043 **$19.99**

Storyteller resources and additional Bible study titles can be found online at lifeway.com/storyteller

Price and availability subject to change without notice.